HOMEMADE FERMENTATION BY MORTIER PILON

MORTIER PILON
BRINGS FERMENTATION
BACK IN THE HOME
KITCHEN

HOMEMADE FERMENTATION
BY **MORTIER PILON**

MortierPilon.com

#PantryCulture

TABLE OF

CONDIMENT™

LACTOFERMENTED SALSA . . . . P 12
LACTOFERMENTED KETCHUP . . . . P 14
FERMENTED RELISH . . . . P 16
FERMENTED GREEN DRESSING . . . . . . P 18
FERMENTED MUSTARD . . . . P 20
FERMENTED CHILI SAUCE . . . . P 22
LACTOFERMENTED MAYONNAISE . . . . . P 24
HORSERADISH . . . . P 26

FERMENTATION™

DILL PICKLES . . . . P 32
FERMENTED GRAPE TOMATOES . . . . . P 34
SPICY CHUTNEY . . . . P 36
LACTOFERMENTED GARLIC . . . . . . P 38
FERMENTED VEGGIE MEDLEY . . . . . . P 40
LACTOFERMENTED CARROTS AND ONIONS . . . P 42
LACTOFERMENTED BEETS . . . . P 44
MOROCCAN LEMON PRESERVES . . . . . . P 46
RED CURTIDO . . . . P 48

KOMBUCHA™

CLASSIC KOMBUCHA . . . . P 54
SPARKLING KOMBUCHA . . . . P 56
STRAWBERRY, BANANA & KOMBUCHA SMOOTHIE . P 58
KOMBUCHA & MAPLE SYRUP VINAIGRETTE . . . . P 60
KOMBUCHA FLU TONIC . . . . P 62
BEET KVASS . . . . P 64
WATER KEFIR . . . . P 66
GINGER BUG SODA . . . . P 68
PROBIOTIC SPARKLING LEMONADE . . . . . . P 70

CONTENTS

KIMCHI BAECHU . . . . P 76

KIMCHIGUK . . . . P 78

KIMCHI JEON . . . . P 80

KIMCHI BOKKEUMBAP . . . . P 82

KIMCHI JJIGAE . . . . P 84

KIMCHI KKAKDUGI . . . . P 86

KIMCHI OI-SOBAGI . . . . P 88

KIMCHI YEOLMU . . . . P 90

DONGCHIMI . . . . P 92

BIBIMBAP . . . . P 94

SIMPLE SAUERKRAUT . . . . P 100

BAVARIAN SAUERKRAUT . . . . P 102

SOUR SHCHI . . . . P 104

POLISH PIEROGI . . . . P 106

CHOUCROUTE GARNIE . . . . P 108

VEPŘO-KNEDLO-ZELO . . . . P 110

PENNSYLVANIA-STYLE PORK ROAST . . . . . . P 112

COUNTRY-STYLE KRAUT & RIBS . . . . . . P 114

CLASSIC REUBEN SANDWICH . . . . P 116

MORTIER — PILON

FERMENTING
LIKE YOU'VE NEVER
DIY'D BEFORE

Mortier Pilon is all about bringing the
fun back to the process of making kombucha,
kimchi, pickles and sauerkraut.

MORTIER
— PILON

KOMBUCHA
HOME BREWING

MortierPilon.com

INTRO

THE BENEFITS OF FERMENTATION

Mortier Pilon draws inspiration from ancient traditions to create home fermentation recipes that will enrich your diet with a wealth of health benefits.

In addition to being cheap and delicious, fermented foods:

1. restore the natural balance of your gut flora;

2. stabilize gastric acidity;

3. facilitate nutrient absorption;

4. contribute to intestinal health;

5. are preserved with no loss of nutritional value;

6. stimulate the immune system.

Unfortunately, most store-bought, industrially made fermented foods are pasteurized, a process during which all microflora—which is at the very core of the health benefits outlined above, and thrives in foods fermented according to tradition—is destroyed.

DUCTION

THE ORIGINS OF FERMENTATION

Strictly speaking, fermentation precedes human history. So the story goes, our ancestors' first attempts at home brewing were inspired by ripe fruit which, having fallen from a tree and remained on the ground for a little while, was going through the early stages of natural fermentation.

The earliest known evidence of alcoholic home brewing dates back as far as 7,000 BC, in the Neolithic village of Jiahu, in China, where villagers were already making a fermented beverage from fruit, rice and honey.

For some of the first civilizations, this mysterious phenomenon was little short of a miracle. As such, the Egyptians worshipped Osiris for their beer, while the Greeks adored Bacchus, the god of winemaking.

Fermentation as a way to preserve food, in contrast, seems to be a relatively recent invention. It appears it was in China, around 200 BC, that human beings first attempted to ferment food. The story goes that salt, having been accidentally sprinkled onto raw vegetables, was later found to have significantly prolonged their edibility—and so fermentation was added to the short list of early food preservation methods, alongside drying, smoking and freezing.

TYPES OF FERMENTATION

Back in the 19th century, Louis Pasteur, considered by many as the founder of present-day microbiology, stated that fermentation was akin to "life without air."

Pasteur's statement had to be nuanced and refined over time; we now define fermentation as a biochemical, anaerobic (without air) reaction which aims to liberate energy via the action of yeasts and bacteria, starting with sugars that are naturally present in food.

These microorganisms decompose organic matter and, through this process, liberate and multiply particles which are highly beneficial for our health.

One can distinguish between three main types of fermentation:

Alcoholic fermentation

Alcoholic fermentation, also called ethyl fermentation, uses certain types of yeasts' ability to transform sugar into ethanol. Our ancestors quickly became familiar with this process as they were learning to brew their own alcohol.

Malolactic fermentation

Malolactic fermentation generally occurs after alcoholic fermentation, once the sugars present in the fermented food have been entirely consumed, and brings about the production of acetic acid. Among other things, this process is used when making vinegar.

Lactic fermentation

Lactic fermentation, finally, transforms sugars into lactic acid through the action of bacteria. It is the key to making yogurt, cheese, cured meats and vegetable pickles.

The following recipes have been developed based on the fermenting technique known as lactic fermentation, also called lactofermentation.

CONDIMENT™

CON —

You can't talk about fermentation without talking about fruits and vegetables. Fermentation has always been, first and foremost, a great, efficient way to preserve crops all year long.

Fruits and vegetables are the perfect starting point for those who want an introduction to fermentation without any of the fuss. Already bursting with flavor at the moment they're picked, they only require careful handling and simple seasoning to transform within a few days into condiments, toppings and snacks, the taste and texture of which will easily rival the store-bought version.

From salsa to horseradish, from mayo to chili sauce, this chapter is filled with recipes to make your own condiments at home. The recipes are simple and the results will amply justify the time spent in the kitchen!

DIMENTS

LACTOFERMENTED SALSA

ACTIVE TIME **TOTAL TIME** **CROCK** **FERMENTATION**

In addition to being finger-licking good, this lactofermented salsa will keep for much longer than its store-bought counterpart.

INGREDIENTS

1½ CUPS (375 ML) **POBLANO PEPPERS**

10 **ROMA TOMATOES**, DICED

¼ CUP (65 ML) DRIED **HERBES DE PROVENCE**

1 TBS (15 ML) **CORIANDER SEEDS**

5 CLOVES **GARLIC**, MINCED

1 LARGE **SPANISH ONION**, MINCED

4 TBS (60 ML) **COARSE SALT**

DIRECTIONS

Chop the peppers, making sure to remove the seeds. In a large bowl, mix together the peppers, tomatoes, herbes de Provence, coriander seeds, garlic and onion.

Transfer the tomato mixture to your Mortier Pilon fermentation jar and press. Cover with salt. Make sure to leave ¾ of an inch (2 centimeters) of headspace between the tomato mixture and the rim of the jar.

Let the mixture ferment at room temperature, covered, for 3 to 5 days. If, after 24 hours, the liquid that has appeared does not cover all of the mixture, add some water and a pinch of salt. Once the desired level of fermentation has been reached, refrigerate or serve.

LACTOFERMENTED KETCHUP

ACTIVE TIME   **TOTAL TIME**   **CROCK**   **FERMENTATION**

This ketchup is so tasty and easy to make that you'll never again want store-bought! Like most fermented condiments, it can be kept in the fridge for months without any risk of going bad.

INGREDIENTS

1 SMALL CAN **TOMATO PASTE**

6 TBS (90 ML) **MAPLE SYRUP**

2 TSP (10 ML) **SALT**

3 TBS (45 ML) **APPLE CIDER VINEGAR**

½ CUP (125 ML) **WHEY**

½ TSP (2.5 ML) **NUTMEG**

¼ TSP (1.25 ML) **CHILI POWDER**

3 **CLOVES**

DIRECTIONS

In a bowl, mix together all the ingredients.

Transfer the mixture to your Mortier Pilon fermentation jar. Make sure to leave ¾ of an inch (2 centimeters) of headspace between the mixture and the rim of the jar.

Let the mixture ferment at room temperature, covered, for 4 days. Serve immediately or store in the refrigerator.

FERMENTED RELISH

Cucumbers, dill and a little salt: as far as fermented condiments go, you can't do much simpler than this one. And yet, after trying this relish, we promise you'll never look back. To make it a little fancier, combine it with a bit of lactofermented mayo (our picture), and you've got a homemade tartare sauce!

5 MIN	5 MIN	2L	4 DAYS
ACTIVE TIME	TOTAL TIME	CROCK	FERMENTATION

INGREDIENTS

6 SMALL **CUCUMBERS**, FINELY CHOPPED

3 TBS (45 ML) **DILL**, CHOPPED

1 TBS (15 ML) **SALT**

DIRECTIONS

In a bowl, combine the cucumbers, dill and salt. Transfer the mixture to your Mortier Pilon jar. Make sure to leave ¾ of an inch (2 centimeters) of headspace between the mixture and the rim of the jar.

Let the mixture ferment at room temperature, covered, for at least 4 days. Once the desired level of fermentation has been reached, refrigerate or serve.

FERMENTED GREEN DRESSING

Fresh cucumbers, flavorful garlic, zesty scallions and a hint of dill from the pickle brine: this vinaigrette truly has it all! Keep a jar in the refrigerator in the summer: we guarantee it'll soon become an inseparable companion to your salads!

ACTIVE TIME   **TOTAL TIME**   **CROCK**   **FERMENTATION**

INGREDIENTS

6 SMALL **CUCUMBERS**,
PEELED AND COARSELY CHOPPED

6 **SCALLIONS**, COARSELY CHOPPED

2 **GARLIC** CLOVES, FINELY CHOPPED

¼ TSP (1.25 ML) **SALT**

¼ TSP (1.25 ML) **DILL PICKLE BRINE**

DIRECTIONS

In a food processor, blend together cucumbers, scallions and garlic until smooth and homogenous, adding a little bit of water to thin as needed. Add in salt and blend some more, then adjust seasoning. Lastly, blend in the brine.

Transfer the mixture to your Mortier Pilon fermentation jar. Let sit to ferment, covered and at room temperatuer, for 3 days. Serve immediately or keep in the refrigerator.

FERMENTED MUSTARD

ACTIVE TIME **TOTAL TIME** **CROCK** **FERMENTATION**

This mustard is not only a hundred times tastier than its store-bought counterpart; it's also packed with essential nutrients! Use it in burgers and sandwiches or serve it alongside sausages and sauerkraut—we promise you won't be disappointed!

INGREDIENTS

½ CUP (125 ML) **MUSTARD POWDER**

3 TBS (45 ML) **WHEY**

2 TBS (30 ML) **WATER**

2 TSP (10 ML) **SEA SALT**

DIRECTIONS

In a bowl, mix together all the ingredients. Transfer the mixture into your Mortier Pilon fermentation jar. Make sure to leave ¾ of an inch (2 centimeters) of headspace between the mixture and the rim of the jar.

Let the mixture ferment at room temperature, covered, for 3 days. Once the desired level of fermentation has been reached, refrigerate or serve.

Serving Suggestion

FERMENTED CHILI SAUCE

ACTIVE TIME   **TOTAL TIME**   **CROCK**   **FERMENTATION**

This sauce is as *picante* as it is colorful! To be used in moderation if you have a sensitive palate, its fresh, complex taste will surprise you.

INGREDIENTS

2 CUPS (500 ML) **CHILI PEPPERS**

2 TSP (10 ML) **COARSE SALT**

½ CUP (125 ML) **APPLE CIDER VINEGAR**

DIRECTIONS

Chop the chili peppers, making sure to remove the seeds. Place the chili peppers in your Mortier Pilon fermentation jar. Cover with salt. Make sure to leave ¾ of an inch (2 centimeters) of headspace between the mixture and the rim of the jar.

Let the mixture ferment at room temperature, covered, for 4 to 5 weeks, or until small bubbles have stopped appearing on the surface. If, after 24 hours, the liquid that has appeared does not cover all of the mixture, add some water and a pinch of salt.

Transfer the fermented chili peppers and the brine to a food processor. Pulse for 3 minutes, or until the mixture is smooth. Add the vinegar and pulse for 30 more seconds to incorporate it into the sauce. Refrigerate or serve.

LACTOFERMENTED MAYONNAISE

ACTIVE TIME   **TOTAL TIME**   **CROCK**   **FERMENTATION**

Store-bought mayonnaise may be practical, but it comes with all sorts of artificial ingredients that are best avoided. But don't worry: this lactofermented mayo can be made in a flash. Plus, it'll be the best you've ever tasted!

INGREDIENTS

1 WHOLE LARGE **EGG**

1 ADDITIONAL **EGG YOLK**

2 TSP (10 ML) **DIJON MUSTARD**

3 TBS (45 ML) **LEMON JUICE**

2 TSP (10 ML) **WHEY**

½ TSP (2.5 ML) **SEA SALT**

½ CUP (125 ML) **GRAPESEED OIL**

½ CUP (125 ML) **CANOLA OIL**

DIRECTIONS

In a food processor, mix at high speed the whole egg, egg yolk, Dijon mustard, lemon juice, whey and sea salt. While continuing to mix, gradually add the grapeseed and canola oil until the mixture thickens.

Transfer the mixture to your Mortier Pilon fermentation jar. Make sure to leave ¾ of an inch (2 centimeters) of headspace between the mixture and the rim of the jar. Let the mixture ferment at room temperature, covered, for 24 hours. Refrigerate or serve.

HORSERADISH

ACTIVE TIME   **TOTAL TIME**   **CROCK**   **FERMENTATION**

This very tasty sauce is also packed with probiotics! Serve it with roasts, and really anywhere you'd use mayonnaise. Be mindful of your eyes when you prepare it, as horseradish root liberates certain irritant volatiles when it is cut.

INGREDIENTS

1½ CUPS (375 ML) **HORSERADISH**

2 TSP (10 ML) **SALT**

⅓ CUP (55 ML) **WHEY**

2 TBS (30 ML) **WATER**

DIRECTIONS

In a food processor, combine the horseradish, salt and whey. Pulse for 1 minute until finely chopped.

Gradually add water and pulse until a doughy texture is achieved.

Transfer the mixture to your Mortier Pilon fermentation jar. Make sure to leave ¾ of an inch (2 centimeters) of headspace between the horseradish mixture and the rim of the jar.

Let the mixture ferment at room temperature, covered, for 1 week. Once the desired level of fermentation has been reached, refrigerate or serve.

Serving Suggestion

FERMENTATION™

PICKLING FERMENTATION CROCK

You can't talk about fermentation without talking about fruits and vegetables. Fermentation has always been, first and foremost, a great, efficient way to preserve crops all year long.

Fruits and vegetables are the perfect starting point for those who want an introduction to fermentation without any of the fuss. Already bursting with flavor at the moment they're picked, they only require careful handling and simple seasoning to transform within a few days into condiments, toppings and snacks, the taste and texture of which will easily rival the store-bought version.

FRUITS & VEGETABLES

The following recipes also feature fermented fruits and veggies. They are crunchy, juicy and filled with flavor. Add them to your sandwiches, use them to decorate your salads, or enjoy them as a snack: they'll be delicious anywhere and for any occasion.

VEGGIE

FERMENTATION

DILL PICKLES

ACTIVE TIME   **TOTAL TIME**   **CROCK**   **FERMENTATION**

5 MIN   2H05   2L   1 WEEK

Crunchy and sour, these pickles are fermented with dill and garlic for a final product that's both fragrant and scrumptious!

INGREDIENTS

3 CUPS (750 ML) **KIRBY CUCUMBERS**

½ BUNCH **DILL**

5 CLOVES **GARLIC**

3 TSP (7.5 ML) **MUSTARD SEEDS**

3 TSP (7.5 ML) **PEPPERCORNS**

4 **CLOVES**

2 TBS (30 ML) **COARSE SALT**

4 CUPS (1L) **WATER**

DIRECTIONS

Soak the cucumbers in water for 2 hours. Scrub and rinse.

Place half of the bunch of dill in your Mortier Pilon fermentation jar. Add the cucumbers and the rest of the dill along with the garlic, mustard seeds, pepper and cloves.

Prepare a brine solution by combining the 8 cups (2L) of water and coarse salt. Add the brine to the jar. Make sure to leave ¾ of an inch (2 centimeters) of headspace between the mixture and the rim of the jar.

Let the mixture ferment at room temperature, covered, for 1 week. Once the desired level of fermentation has been reached, refrigerate or serve.

FERMENTED GRAPE TOMATOES

ACTIVE TIME   **TOTAL TIME**   **CROCK**   **FERMENTATION**

This deceptively simple recipe will allow you to enjoy the most summery of combinations during the cold winter months, when the fresh, flavorful tomatoes and basil of the warmer season are long gone.

INGREDIENTS

4 CUPS (1L) **GRAPE TOMATOES**, WASHED AND HULLED

4 CUPS (1L) **WATER**

4 TBS (60 ML) **SALT**

FRESH **BASIL LEAVES**

DIRECTIONS

Poke each tomato with a toothpick to allow the brine to penetrate the skin. Place the prepared tomatoes in your Mortier Pilon fermentation jar.

Insert a basil leaf between the tomatoes every inch (3 or 4 centimeters). Cover the mixture with salt. Make sure to leave ¾ of an inch (2 centimeters) of headspace between the tomatoes and the rim of the jar.

Let the mixture ferment at room temperature, covered, for at least 4 days. If, after 24 hours, the liquid that has appeared does not cover all of the mixture, add some water and a pinch of salt. Once the desired level of fermentation has been reached, refrigerate or serve.

SPICY CHUTNEY

ACTIVE TIME   **TOTAL TIME**   **CROCK**   **FERMENTATION**

At once spicy, fruity and a touch exotic, this chutney might surprise you! Very colorful and highly adaptable, you can feel free to personalize it by subbing the peaches with pears or plums!

INGREDIENTS

2 **JALAPEÑO PEPPERS**

2 RIPE **PEACHES**, DICED

2 RED **APPLES**, DICED

¼ CUP (65 ML) **WALNUTS**

½ CUP (125 ML) **POMEGRANATE SEEDS**

4 TSP (20 ML) **SALT**

JUICE OF 2 FRESH **LEMONS**

2 TSP (10 ML) GRATED **GINGER ROOT**

WATER, FOR COVERING THE MIXTURE

DIRECTIONS

Chop the peppers, making sure to remove the seeds. In a bowl, combine the salt, ginger and peppers.

Place the peaches and apples in your Mortier Pilon fermentation jar. Add the walnuts, pomegranate seeds, spice mixture and lemon juice. Mix and add water. Make sure to leave ¾ of an inch (2 centimeters) of headspace between the mixture and the rim of the jar.

Let the mixture ferment at room temperature, covered, for 3 days. If, after 24 hours, the liquid does not cover all of the mixture, add some water and a pinch of salt. Once the desired level of fermentation has been reached, refrigerate or serve.

LACTOFERMENTED GARLIC

Everyone loves garlic (well, almost everyone). The only trouble is, since raw garlic's taste is too pronounced for most palates, most of us tend to fry it or roast it; in both cases, the result is delicious, however most of the enzymes and nutrients found in the raw product are lost in the cooking process. Fermentation, on the other hand, allows you to enjoy garlic while preserving its tremendous nutritional value.

ACTIVE TIME

TOTAL TIME

CROCK

FERMENTATION

INGREDIENTS

16 CLOVES **GARLIC**, PEELED

4 CUPS (1L) **BRINE**

2 **BAY LEAVES**

1 TBS (15 ML) **HERBES DE PROVENCE**

DIRECTIONS

Place the garlic cloves in your Mortier Pilon fermentation jar.

Add the brine, bay leaves and herbes de Provence. Make sure to leave ¾ of an inch (2 centimeters) of headspace between the mixture and the rim of the jar.

Let the mixture ferment at room temperature, covered, for 1 month. Once the desired level of fermentation has been reached, refrigerate or serve.

ACTIVE TIME   **TOTAL TIME**   **CROCK**   **FERMENTATION**

VEGETABLE MEDLEY

Hurray for veggie medleys! This combination of cucumbers, carrots, leek and cauliflower is tasty, colorful and packed with vitamins.

INGREDIENTS

3 **PEARS**, PEELED AND DICED

3 CUPS (750 ML) **CAULIFLOWER**

2 CUPS (500 ML) **CARROTS**, PEELED AND DICED

1 **LEEK**, SLICED

3 TBS (45 ML) **GINGER ROOT**, MINCED

¼ CUP (65 ML) **SALT**

DIRECTIONS

In a large bowl, combine all of the ingredients except the salt.

Place the mixture in your Mortier Pilon fermentation jar and press. Make sure to leave ¾ of an inch (2 centimeters) of headspace between the vegetable mixture and the rim of the jar. Cover with salt.

Let the mixture ferment at room temperature, covered, for 3 to 5 days. If, after 24 hours, the liquid that has appeared does not cover all of the mixture, add some water and a pinch of salt. Once the desired level of fermentation has been reached, refrigerate or serve.

Serving Suggestion

LACTOFERMENTED CARROTS AND ONIONS

ACTIVE TIME **TOTAL TIME** **CROCK** **FERMENTATION**

Pearl onions and carrot half-moons are an elegant, colorful addition to your salads, appetizers and cocktails. Plus, they're filled with vitamins!

INGREDIENTS

10 LARGE **CARROTS**,
CUT INTO ROUNDS OR HALF-MOONS

30 **PEARL ONIONS**

4 CUPS (1L) **BRINE**

DIRECTIONS

Combine the onions and carrots in your Mortier Pilon fermentation jar. Add the brine. Make sure to leave ¾ of an inch (2 centimeters) of headspace between the carrot mixture and the rim of the jar.

Let the mixture ferment at room temperature, covered, for 1 week. Once the desired level of fermentation has been reached, refrigerate or serve.

LACTOFERMENTED BEETS

ACTIVE TIME **TOTAL TIME** **CROCK** **FERMENTATION**

These fermented beet slices are as delicious as they are easy to make. Tuck them in sandwiches, add them to salads or just eat them as a snack! They'll taste amazing everywhere.

INGREDIENTS

2 CUPS (500 ML) **BEETS**, SLICED

2 TBS (30 ML) **COARSE SALT**

4 CUPS (1L) **WATER**

DIRECTIONS

Place the beets in your Mortier Pilon fermentation jar.

Prepare a brine solution by combining the water and coarse salt. Add the brine to the jar. Make sure to leave ¾ of an inch (2 centimeters) of headspace between the beets and the rim of the jar.

Let the mixture ferment at room temperature, covered, for 1 week. Once the desired level of fermentation has been reached, refrigerate or serve.

MOROCCAN LEMON PRESERVES

ACTIVE TIME **TOTAL TIME** **CROCK** **FERMENTATION**

Lemon preserves are a staple of Northern African cooking. Both sour and salty, they are the perfect addition to tajine, couscous and roast chicken. Plus, with only two ingredients, they couldn't be easier to make!

INGREDIENTS

10 **LEMONS**

⅓ CUP (55 ML) **COARSE SALT**

DIRECTIONS

Cut off one of the ends of each lemon, leaving as much flesh remaining as possible. Make 2 lengthwise slashes on each lemon, making sure to leave the quarters joined at the other end of the lemon.

Sprinkle each lemon generously with salt. Place the lemons one by one in your Mortier Pilon fermentation jar, gently crushing to release the juice. Repeat this step until all of the lemons are in the jar. The juice should cover all of the lemons. Make sure to leave ¾ of an inch (2 centimeters) of headspace between the lemons and the rim of the jar.

Let the mixture ferment at room temperature, covered, for 3 to 4 weeks. Once the desired level of fermentation has been reached, refrigerate or serve.

RED CURTIDO

ACTIVE TIME   **TOTAL TIME**   **CROCK**   **FERMENTATION**

Part salad and part relish, this not-so-distant relative of sauerkraut is made of fermented cabbage (red cabbage in our case) and fermented carrots. It's often served as a side to pupusa, a type of thick, corn-based pancake.

INGREDIENTS

2 CUPS (500 ML) SHREDDED **RED CABBAGE**

¼ CUP (65 ML) GRATED **CARROTS**

2 TBS (30 ML) **CHIVES**

BOILING **WATER**, FOR COVERING THE MIXTURE

⅓ CUP (55 ML) **CIDER VINEGAR**

⅓ CUP (55 ML) **WATER**

A PINCH **CHILI POWDER**

1 TSP (5 ML) **SALT**

GROUND **BLACK PEPPER**, TO TASTE

DIRECTIONS

In a glass bowl, combine the cabbage, carrots and chives. Cover with boiling water and set aside.

In a bowl, mix together the cider vinegar, water, chili powder, salt and pepper. Drain the vegetables and place them in your Mortier Pilon fermentation jar.

Add the vinaigrette and mix. Let the mixture rest at room temperature for 3 hours. Serve or refrigerate.

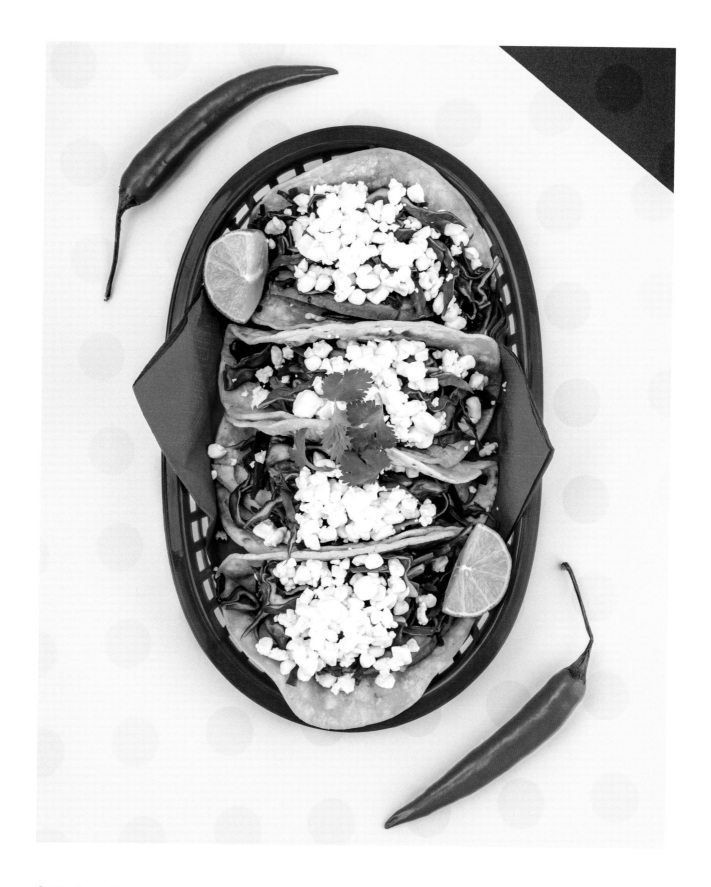

The pages that follow contain everything you need to know to start brewing your own lactofermented beverages right at home. And though kombucha is featured prominently here, the advice applies to most other fermented drinks as well.

WHAT IS KOMBUCHA?

Kombucha is a fermented tea that's packed with vitamins, antioxidants and probiotics, making it both delicious and good for you. It's a living drink made by fermenting sweetened tea using a kombucha culture, or SCOBY, which stands for symbiotic culture of bacteria and yeast. As the SCOBY "digests" the sugar in the tea, it generates a variety of probiotics, enzymes and amino acids, turning the initial tea into a nutrient-packed, tangy, effervescent health drink that's also deliciously addictive.

Only four ingredients are required to make kombucha: water, tea, sugar and a kombucha culture (SCOBY). Selecting the right ingredients is key to creating a healthy environment for your SCOBY to grow, and to a quality final product.

Water must be free from chlorine as well as all contaminants. Use filtered water or boil tap water for at least 20 minutes before using.

The type of tea used is also important, as it will affect your SCOBY's health as well as the taste of the final product. Choose an organic tea to avoid contaminants. Black and oolong teas are recommended, although for a more mild-tasting kombucha, you can use green tea as well. Always avoid teas containing oils or added flavors.

Sugar is essential to the fermentation process; do not omit it or try to use another ingredient in its place. Use too little sugar in your mix and your SCOBY might starve! White cane sugar and sugarcane juice are recommended. Brown sugar, honey and other syrups tend to give less reliable results, while artificial sweeteners do not constitute a sufficient source of nutrients for your SCOBY.

Use a fresh SCOBY to start a new infusion: the results obtained with a dehydrated SCOBY will be far less reliable. Do not use hot water, as it might kill the SCOBY; room-temperature liquid will work best.

KOM — BUCHA

10 MIN ACTIVE TIME **1H00** TOTAL TIME **5L** CROCK **5 DAYS** FERMENTATION

CLASSIC KOMBUCHA

1 | Helping your SCOBY Acclimate to its New Environment

Before you can brew your first batch of kombucha, make sure your SCOBY settles in its new environment. Attempting to immediately start making large quantities of kombucha with a new SCOBY could result in your colony of microorganisms dying, so make sure to take things slow at first.

In order to avoid contamination, it is key to first clean your Mortier Pilon fermentation jar. To sterilize the jar:

1. Put it in the dishwasher for a run, or clean by hand using very hot water and a mild soap.

2. Leave it to dry overnight on a dry, clean towel. Avoid touching the inside of the jar, including with the towel.

These next few steps will allow your SCOBY to truly settle into its new environment:

1. Heat 4 cups (1 L) of filtered water. Place 3 bags of organic tea (preferably black or oolong) in the hot water.

2. Add ½ a cup (125 ml) of white sugar (avoid brown sugar and honey).

3. Let the mixture cool (your SCOBY doesn't like the heat!).

4. Pour room-temperature sweetened tea into your sterilized Mortier Pilon fermentation jar.

5. Place your SCOBY in the jar; make sure to include the juice from the sachet as well.

6. Cover and let sit for 2 to 3 days.

2 | Primary Fermentation

Once your SCOBY has settled into its new environment, it can start producing larger quantities of kombucha.

During this first fermentation stage, the SCOBY will feed on sugar and liberate carbon dioxide. At this step, the gas will pass through the porous wall of the Mortier Pilon jar, resulting in a still (non-sparkling) drink.

With time and as the fermentation process goes on, the drink will become less and less sweet.

To brew a large quantity of kombucha for the first time, add the following to your initial brew:

1. Heat 3 L of filtered water. Place 5 bags of organic tea (preferably black or oolong) in the hot water.

2. Add 2 cups (500 ml) of white sugar (avoid brown sugar and honey).

3. Let the mixture cool (your SCOBY doesn't like the heat!).

4. Pour room-temperature sweetened tea into your sterilized Mortier Pilon fermentation jar.

5. Cover and let sit for a week, then taste. For a drink that's less sweet, let sit for another few days or up to 2 weeks.

The SCOBY feeds on the sugar and the gas is evacuated through the jar's porous wall.

ACTIVE TIME **TOTAL TIME** **SWINGTOP** **FERMENTATION**

10 MIN 10 MIN 315 ML 2 WEEKS

SPARKLING KOMBUCHA

3 | Secondary Fermentation and Flavor Additions

It is secondary fermentation that will make your kombucha fizzy. It is also at this step that you can incorporate new flavors into your brew. To do so:

1. Transfer the kombucha into one or several Mortier Pilon flip-top bottles.

2. Add in about ½ tablespoon (7.5 ml)) of sugar per bottle.

3. Add in fruit slices, fruit juice, fresh herbs or spices. (This step is optional.)

4. Make sure to shut the lid.

5. Let sit for 4 to 5 days. The longer this step, the fizzier the kombucha.

6. Filter, then enjoy!

There are lots of ways to get creative with your kombucha! To find out what your favorite ingredient combination is, experimenting is the best method. Nonetheless, feel free to use these flavor pairing ideas:

1. Mango & Apricot

2. Strawberry & Lemonade

3. Coconut & Pineapple

4. Ginger & Turmeric

5. Apple & Cinnamon

6. Watermelon & Jalapeño

7. Raspberry & Blueberry

8. Cherry & Vanilla

The SCOBY feeds on the sugar and the gas is evacuated through the jar's porous wall.

STRAWBERRY, BANANA & KOMBUCHA SMOOTHIE

ACTIVE TIME   **TOTAL TIME**

This incredibly fresh smoothie relies on a classic combination (strawberries and bananas) and the slightly spicy taste of fizzy kombucha to bring you a drink that is all at once colorful, thirst-quenching and energizing.

INGREDIENTS

1 CUP (250 ML) **KOMBUCHA**

1 RIPE **BANANA**

½ CUP (125 ML) FROZEN **STRAWBERRIES** AND **BLACKBERRIES**

DIRECTIONS

In a blender, mix all of the ingredients at high speed until smooth. Serve immediately in a tall glass.

KOMBUCHA & MAPLE SYRUP VINAIGRETTE

Here's a well-kept secret: kombucha is a great replacement for vinegar in most raw condiment recipes. Don't hesitate to add it to your favorite vinaigrettes and sauces for a probiotic kick in your next salad!

ACTIVE TIME   **TOTAL TIME**

INGREDIENTS

⅓ CUP (55 ML) **KOMBUCHA**

2 TBS (30 ML) **ORANGE JUICE**

2 TBS (30 ML) **MAPLE SYRUP**

2 TSP (10 ML) **SALT**

A PINCH **BLACK PEPPER**

1 CUP (250 ML) EXTRA-VIRGIN **OLIVE OIL**

DIRECTIONS

In a food processor, mix together the first 5 ingredients for 1 minute.

Gradually add the oil, if possible while continuing to mix. Serve immediately or refrigerate.

KOMBUCHA
FLU TONIC

ACTIVE TIME   **TOTAL TIME**   **CROCK**   **FERMENTATION**

One of the most important benefits of fermented foods—and especially of kombucha—is their ability to stimulate our immune system. This kombucha tonic is a great way to use kombucha that may have fermented longer and developed a vinegary taste.

INGREDIENTS

2 TBS (30 ML) **KOMBUCHA VINEGAR**

1 TSP (5 ML) GRATED **GINGER ROOT**

½ TSP (2.5 ML) **HORSERADISH**

1 SMALL **ONION**, CHOPPED

1 TSP (5 ML) GRATED **WHITE RADISH**

3 CLOVES **GARLIC**, PRESSED

1 SMALL **JALAPEÑO PEPPER**, CHOPPED

A PINCH **CAYENNE PEPPER**

2 TSP (10 ML) **TURMERIC**

DIRECTIONS

Place all of the ingredients in your Mortier Pilon fermentation jar. Let the mixture ferment at room temperature, covered, for 1 month. The longer the mixture ferments, the stronger it will be.

Once the desired concentration has been reached, filter the mixture using a sieve. Store in the refrigerator.

Drink 2 tsp (10 ml) of tonic daily.

BEET KVASS

5 MIN
ACTIVE TIME

5 MIN
TOTAL TIME

2L
CROCK

3 DAYS
FERMENTATION

Kvass is a Slavic fermented drink traditionally made from stale bread. This version uses beets to deliver a beautiful, purple juice which is delicious both straight up and as a dressing in your favorite salad.

INGREDIENTS

6 **BEETS**, PEELED AND SLICED

2 CUPS (500ML) **WATER**

4 TSP (20 ML) **SALT**

DIRECTIONS

Mix together the beets and salt and place them in your Mortier Pilon fermentation jar. Cover with water and stir to dissolve the salt.

Let the mixture ferment at room temperature, covered, for 3 days. To serve, pour desired amount of kvas into a glass.

ACTIVE TIME **TOTAL TIME** **CROCK** **FERMENTATION**

WATER KEFIR

This probiotic-rich, irresistibly fruity water kefir is endlessly customizable to boot.

INGREDIENTS

50 TO 70 **KEFIR GRAINS**, REHYDRATED

4 CUPS (1L) ROOM TEMPERATURE **WATER**

¼ CUP (65 ML) **CANE SUGAR**

¼ CUP (65 ML) **FRUIT JUICE** (SUCH AS GRAPE OR APPLE)

DIRECTIONS

In a pan, heat ½ a cup (125 ml) of water without bringing it to a boil. Add the sugar and stir until it dissolves. Remove from heat and let cool until the liquid has reached room temperature.

Pour the sugar/water mixture, followed by the rest of the water, into your Mortier Pilon fermentation jar. Add the kefir grains. Let the mixture ferment at room temperature, covered, for 2 days.

After 2 days, filter the kefir water using a bamboo strainer (avoid metal if possible). Transfer to Mortier Pilon swing-top bottles.

Distribute the fruit juice among the bottles and let the kefir ferment for 2 days for more carbonation.

GINGER BUG SODA

ACTIVE TIME **TOTAL TIME** **CROCK** **FERMENTATION**

This homebrewed drink is just as a fizzy and tasty as store-bought soda! Plus, it's packed with good bacteria sure to heal your stomach and boost your immune system.

INGREDIENTS

4 TBS (60 ML) GRATED **GINGER ROOT**

2 TBS (30 ML) **CANE SUGAR**

4 CUPS (1L) **WATER**

½ CUP (125 ML) ROOM TEMPERATURE **FRUIT JUICE** OR **TEA**, ANY KIND

DIRECTIONS

Place 2 tbs (30 ml) ginger root, 1 tbs (15 ml) sugar and 2 cups (500 ml) water in your Mortier Pilon fermentation jar. Stir. Let the mixture ferment at room temperature, covered, for 1 week. Mix in the rest of the ginger, sugar and water. Let the mixture ferment at room temperature, covered, for another week.

Mix ¼ a cup (65 ml) of the ginger bug prepared in step 1 with ½ a cup (125 ml) of juice or tea. Transfer the mixture to Mortier Pilon swing-top bottles. Let the soda ferment for another 4 days in the refrigerator.

PROBIOTIC SPARKLING LEMONADE

ACTIVE TIME **TOTAL TIME** **CROCK** **FERMENTATION**

This next-generation lemonade is both refreshing and packed with probiotics—just what your body needs on long, hot summer afternoons.

INGREDIENTS

5 **LEMONS**

1 TSP (5 ML) **CANE SUGAR**

1 TSP (5 ML) **WHEY**

4 CUPS (1L) **WATER**

DIRECTIONS

Juice the lemons. Transfer the juice to your Mortier Pilon fermentation jar. Add the sugar, whey and a small amount of water. Mix.

Add the rest of the water. Make sure to leave 2 inches (5 centimeters) of headspace between the mixture and the rim of the jar.

Let the mixture ferment at room temperature, covered, for 5 days. Refrigerate or serve.

Kimchi is a Korean fermented dish made of vegetables and a broad variety of seasonings. While dozens of variations exist, most kimchi recipes use nappa cabbage, radishes or cucumbers as their base. Among the most popular seasonings are brine, scallions, red peppers, garlic, saeujeot (a shrimp-based sauce) and aekjeot (a type of fish sauce).

Types of kimchi obviously vary depending on the ingredients used, but their region of origin and the season in which they are prepared also play their part. For example, contrary to the kimchi traditionally made in South Korea, which is very generous in salt and red peppers, North Korean kimchi tends to be both less salty and less spicy; likewise, seafood-based brine, which is very popular in the South, is usually left out in the North.

Different types of kimchi are consumed throughout the year, depending primarily on the climate and ingredient availability. And while refrigeration now allows more control over the different stages of fermentation, Koreans as a whole remain attached to their traditions, and as such, there has been little to no change as far as kimchi consumption habits go.

Summer kimchi, which is made using seasonal vegetables, is usually very fresh. After summer, a period of a few weeks follows, which coincides with the year's tenth moon, during which kimchi is prepared in large quantities in anticipation of the cold winter months. For the families that partake in this tradition, called Gimjam, it is the perfect occasion to spend meaningful time together.

KIM —— CHI

KIMCHI BAECHU
(NAPPA CABBAGE KIMCHI)

20 MIN   **3H15**   **2L**   **4 DAYS**

ACTIVE TIME   TOTAL TIME   CROCK   FERMENTATION

Kimchi Baechu is primarily made of fermented nappa cabbage and hot peppers. It also happens to be the most popular winter kimchi. The seasoning varies from one region to another, and is generally saltier, spicier and juicier in the South of Korea.

INGREDIENTS

3 LARGE HEADS **NAPPA CABBAGE**

½ CUP (125 ML) **SALT**

2 ½ CUPS (625 ML) **WATER**

3 TBS (45 ML) **WHITE RICE FLOUR**

1 TBS (15 ML) **CANE SUGAR**

5 CLOVES **GARLIC**, FINELY CHOPPED

3 TBS (45 ML) **GINGER ROOT**, MINCED

1 SMALL **ONION**, CHOPPED

½ CUP (125 ML) **FISH SAUCE**

⅓ CUP (55 ML) **SALTED FERMENTED SHRIMP**

½ CUP (125 ML) **KOREAN CHILI PEPPER**

1 MEDIUM **DAIKON RADISH**,
PEELED AND JULIENNED

4 **CARROTS**, PEELED AND JULIENNED

6 **SCALLIONS**, CHOPPED

½ CUP (125 ML) **CHINESE CHIVES**,
FINELY CHOPPED

DIRECTIONS

Cut the cabbage in half, making sure not to damage the inner leaves. Make a lengthwise slash on each cabbage half, making sure not to cut all the way to the core. The leaves should be attached to the core but able to move.

Fill a large bowl with water. Immerse the cabbage in the water for several seconds. Remove the cabbage and sprinkle generously with salt, including the spaces betweens the leaves that are hard to see. If the leaves are thick, add salt near the core.

Cover with a clean cloth and let stand at room temperature for at least 3 hours. Meanwhile, prepare the rice porridge. In a small pan, combine the 2 ½ cups (625 ml) of water with the white rice flour. Mix with a spatula and cook over medium heat until the mixture starts to simmer. Remove from heat and blend in the sugar. Let cool.

Once the mixture has cooled, blend in the garlic, ginger, onion, fish sauce, fermented shrimp and chili pepper. Mix well. Mix in the radish, carrots, scallions and Chinese chives.

After the cabbage has rested for 3 hours, rinse it to remove all of the salt. Cut the cabbage halves into quarters, remove the core and drain completely in a colander.

Spread the kimchi paste on the cabbage leaves. Place the cabbage in your Mortier Pilon fermentation jar. Make sure to leave ¾ of an inch (2 centimeters) of headspace between the cabbage and the rim of the jar. Let the mixture ferment at room temperature, covered, for 4 days before serving.

KIMCHIGUK

(KIMCHI SOUP)

This kimchi baechu-based Korean soup is packed with flavor, easy to make and protein-rich, which makes it the perfect meal for those long winter nights.

ACTIVE TIME **TOTAL TIME**

INGREDIENTS

1½ CUPS (375 ML) **KIMCHI BAECHU**, ROUGHLY CHOPPED

¼ CUP (65 ML) **KIMCHI JUICE**

1 SMALL **ONION**, ROUGHLY CHOPPED

0.66 LB (300 GRAMS) **PORK BELLY**, CUT INTO PIECES

2 TBS (30 ML) **GOJUCHANG**

1 TSP (5 ML) **CANE SUGAR**

4 CUPS (1L) **WATER**

1 LB (400 GRAMS) EXTRA-FIRM **TOFU**, CUBED

3 **SCALLIONS**, SLICED

2 CUPS (500 ML) COOKED **JASMINE RICE**, FOR SERVING

DIRECTIONS

In a large pan, combine the kimchi, kimchi juice, onion, gojuchang, meat and sugar. Add the water. Bring to a boil and cook over high heat for 30 minutes.

Add the tofu and cook for 15 more minutes. Stir in the scallions, reserving a small handful for garnish. Serve with rice.

KIMCHI JEON

(KIMCHI PANCAKES)

These kimchi pancakes are delicious both as a snack and as an appetizer. Plus, they'll be ready in a snap, and to boot, they're a great way to use kimchi that has fermented a bit too long and has developed a strong, pungent taste.

ACTIVE TIME   **TOTAL TIME**

INGREDIENTS

4 **EGGS**

4 CUPS (1L) ALL-PURPOSE **FLOUR**

3 CUPS (750 ML) COLD **WATER**

3 CUPS (750 ML) **BAECHU KIMCHI**

½ CUP (125 ML) **KIMCHI JUICE**

2 TSP (10 ML) **SALT**

2 **SCALLIONS**, CHOPPED

4 TBS (60 ML) **SOY SAUCE**

2 TBS (30 ML) **RICE VINEGAR**

2 TBS (30 ML) **SESAME OIL**

1 TBS (15 ML) **SUGAR**

1 TBS (15 ML) **SESAME SEEDS**

¼ TSP (1.25 ML) **CHILI POWDER**

DIRECTIONS

Whisk the eggs together in a small bowl. In a large bowl, combine the beaten eggs, flour, water, kimchi, kimchi juice and salt.

Cook as you would pancakes, over medium heat in an oiled nonstick pan. Cook each pancake for 2 minutes on each side, until crisp.

In a small bowl, combine all of the other ingredients. Serve the pancakes whole or cut into pieces, with the sauce.

KIMCHI BOKKEUMBAP

(KIMCHI FRIED RICE)

This kimchi fried rice is extremely versatile, which may be the reason it has long been a staple of Korean family cooking. Both the meat and vegetables can be subbed to suit your tastes and budget; just make sure you use kimchi baechu to keep it authentic!

ACTIVE TIME   **TOTAL TIME**

INGREDIENTS

2 **SCALLIONS**

1 TBS (15 ML) **SESAME OIL**

⅓ CUP (55 ML) **PORK** OR **CHICKEN**, CUT INTO PIECES

3 CUPS (750 ML) COOKED **JASMINE RICE**, COOLED

1 TBS (15 ML) **VEGETABLE OIL**

1½ CUPS (375 ML) **KIMCHI BAECHU**, CHOPPED

¼ CUP (65 ML) **KIMCHI JUICE**

1 TBS (15 ML) **SESAME OIL**

2 TSP (10 ML) **SOY SAUCE**

2 **EGGS**

1 TBS (15 ML) **SESAME SEEDS**, FOR SERVING

FRESH **VEGETABLES**, FOR SERVING

DIRECTIONS

Slice the scallions and separate the white parts from the green parts.

Sauté the meat in the oil for 3 to 5 minutes, until the desired doneness is reached. Meanwhile, in a large bowl, combine the rice and vegetable oil with your hands, making sure not to crush the rice.

After the meat has been cooked, mix in the white parts of the sliced scallions and cook them with the meat for 30 seconds. Add the kimchi and kimchi juice and stir. Incorporate the rice and cook the mixture for 8 to 10 minutes, stirring often.

Add the sesame oil and soy sauce and stir. Cook for 4 to 6 more minutes, stirring often. Meanwhile, pan-fry the eggs. Add the green parts of the scallions, reserving a small amount for garnish.

To serve, divide the fried rice between two bowls and top each bowl with a fried egg. Garnish with the reserved scallions and the sesame seeds.

KIMCHI JJIGAE

(KIMCHI STEW)

Kimchi jjigae can be eaten with a variety of sides depending on your taste; just make sure you serve it with rice! For this recipe, we recommend you use older, riper kimchi with a strong smell, as this will translate into the dish and give it lots of spicy, full-bodied flavor.

10 MIN

ACTIVE TIME

35 MIN

TOTAL TIME

INGREDIENTS

2 CUPS (500 ML) **KIMCHI BAECHU**

5 OZ **PORK BELLY**

2 TSP (10 ML) **KOREAN PEPPER FLAKES**

2 TSP (10 ML) CHOPPED **GARLIC**

1 TSP (5 ML) CHOPPED **GINGER ROOT**

⅓ CUP (55 ML) **KIMCHI JUICE**

2 CUPS (500 ML) **WATER**

7 OZ (200 G) EXTRA-FIRM **TOFU**, SLICED INTO ¾-INCH (2 CM) SLABS

3 **SCALLIONS**

SALT AND **PEPPER**, TO TASTE

DIRECTIONS

Cut the kimchi and meat into bite-sized pieces. Cook on medium-high heat in a large pot with the pepper flakes, garlic and ginger, stirring every now and then, until the meat is cooked.

Add in the kimchi juice and water, lower the heat and simmer for 25 minutes. Add water if the stew seems to be getting too thick.

Cut the tofu into half-inch thick slabs and slice the scallions to your liking. Add both to the pot and season.

Simmer, covered, for 5 more minutes or until the tofu is cooked. Serve in the center of the table with rice on the side.

KIMCHI KKAKDUGI

(CUBED RADISH KIMCHI)

To make this kimchi, which is very similar to Kimchi Baechu, nappa cabbage is swapped for daikon radishes. A mixture of fermented shrimp is sometimes added in, giving the kimchi a strong smell and a beautiful dark color.

10 MIN   **1H10**   **2L**   **4 DAYS**

ACTIVE TIME   **TOTAL TIME**   **CROCK**   **FERMENTATION**

INGREDIENTS

2 LARGE **DAIKON RADISHES**, PEELED

3 TSP (15 ML) **CANE SUGAR**

4 TSP (20 ML) **SALT**

⅓ CUP (55 ML) **FISH SAUCE**

½ CUP (125 ML) **HOT PEPPER FLAKES**

3 **SCALLIONS**, SLICED

3 LARGE CLOVES **GARLIC**, CHOPPED

1 TBS (15 ML) **GINGER ROOT**, CHOPPED

DIRECTIONS

Cut the radishes lengthwise into quarters, then cut into 2-centimeter cubes. Rinse and put into a bowl.

Add the salt and sugar and combine. Let the mixture stand at room temperature for 1 hour.

Drain the radishes in a colander, making sure to collect the juice in a bowl. Add the fish sauce, hot pepper flakes, scallions, garlic and ginger to the bowl and mix. Add the radishes and mix, coating them completely in the brine solution.

Place the seasoned radish mixture in your Mortier Pilon fermentation jar. Make sure to leave ¾ of an inch (2 centimeters) of headspace between the radish mixture and the rim of the jar. Let the mixture ferment at room temperature, covered, for 4 days before serving.

KIMCHI OI-SOBAGI
(CUCUMBER KIMCHI)

Kimchi Oi-sobagi's crunchy texture and refreshing taste have made this dish a favorite among summer kimchis. It's made by inserting seasoned vegetables into a cucumber cut lengthwise, making it a delicious vehicle for flavor. This kimchi does not need to be fermented before eating.

ACTIVE TIME   **TOTAL TIME**

15 MIN   45 MIN

INGREDIENTS

8 **KIRBY CUCUMBERS**
(OR 12 LEBANESE CUCUMBERS)

3 TBS (45 ML) **SALT**

½ CUP (125 ML) **CHINESE CHIVES**, CHOPPED

3 CLOVES **GARLIC**, MINCED

3 **CARROTS**, PEELED AND JULIENNED

1 **ONION**, FINELY CHOPPED

⅓ CUP (55 ML) **KOREAN CHILI POWDER**

4 TSP (20 ML) **FISH SAUCE**

2 TBS (30 ML) **CANE SUGAR**

2 TSP (10 ML) **BLACK SESAME SEEDS** (OPTIONAL)

DIRECTIONS

Make 2 lengthwise slashes on each cucumber, making sure to leave the 4 resulting strips attached. Place the cucumbers in a large bowl and sprinkle with salt. Rub each cucumber (the exterior and the flesh) with the salt. Let the cucumbers rest for 30 minutes, turning them halfway through.

While the cucumbers are resting, combine in a bowl the Chinese chives, garlic, carrots, onion, chili powder, fish sauce, sugar and sesame seeds. Set aside.

After the cumbers have rested, rinse them to remove all of the salt and drain them in a colander.

Stuff the cucumbers with the mixture prepared earlier. Contact with chili powder can irritate skin, so wear gloves for this step.

Serve the stuffed cucumbers immediately (this kimchi doesn't need to be fermented) or store in the refrigerator for up to 5 days.

Serving Suggestion

KIMCHI YEOLMU

(YOUNG SUMMER RADISH KIMCHI)

25 MIN   **1H25**   **2L**   **2 DAYS**

ACTIVE TIME   TOTAL TIME   CROCK   FERMENTATION

As small as they are delicious, summer radishes are a seasonal Korean favorite. This dish is often served with rice or cold noodles.

INGREDIENTS

2.2 LB (1 KILO) **YOUNG SUMMER RADISHES**, PEELED

⅔ CUP (170 ML) **SALT**

½ CUP (125 ML) **WATER**

2 TSP (10 ML) **WHITE RICE FLOUR**

2 TBS (30 ML) **CANE SUGAR**

3 CLOVES **GARLIC**, MINCED

1 SMALL PIECE **GINGER ROOT**, FINELY CHOPPED

1 SMALL **ONION**, FINELY CHOPPED

2 **GREEN HOT PEPPERS**

2 **RED HOT PEPPERS**

3 TBS (45 ML) **HOT PEPPER FLAKES**

4 TBS (60 ML) **FISH SAUCE**

6 CUPS (1.5 L) **WATER**

DIRECTIONS

Cut the radishes into small rectangular pieces about 2 inches (5 centimeters) long. Rinse with cold water and drain in a colander.

Once the radishes have been drained, put them in a bowl and mix with the salt. Let the mixture rest at room temperature for 1 hour, stirring once halfway through.

While the radishes are resting, prepare the rice porridge. In a small pan, combine ½ of a cup (125 ml) of water and the white rice flour. Mix with a spatula and cook over medium heat until the mixture starts to simmer. Remove from heat and blend in the sugar. Let cool.

After the radishes have rested, rinse them to remove all of the salt and drain them in a colander. While the radishes are draining, prepare the kimchi paste. In a bowl, mix together the garlic, ginger and onion. Chop the chili peppers, making sure to remove the seeds. Add them to the bowl with the hot pepper flakes, fish sauce and porridge. Mix vigorously.

Add the radishes to the same bowl and mix until they are coated in the kimchi mixture. Place the radish mixture in your Mortier Pilon fermentation jar and add 6 cups (1.5 L) of water. Make sure to leave ¾ of an inch (2 centimeters) of headspace between the radishes and the rim of the jar. Let the mixture ferment at room temperature, covered, for 2 days before serving.

Serving Suggestion

DONGCHIMI

(WATER RADISH KIMCHI)

ACTIVE TIME   TOTAL TIME   CROCK   FERMENTATION

As its name—which literally means winter kimchi—suggests, this kimchi is traditionally made shortly before the beginning of winter, as radishes picked during this time are at their firmest and sweetest.

INGREDIENTS

24 SMALL **WHITE RADISHES** WITH LEAVES

½ CUP (125 ML) **SALT**

6 CLOVES **GARLIC**, CHOPPED

1 SMALL PIECE **GINGER ROOT**, CHOPPED

4 **CHILI PEPPERS**

3 SMALL **SWEET PEARS**, CUBED

4 **SCALLIONS**, SLICED

1 SMALL **ONION**, CUBED

1 TO 2 CUPS (ABOUT 400 ML) **WATER**

CHEESECLOTH

NOODLES, FOR SERVING

DIRECTIONS

Remove the radish leaves and set aside. In a bowl, mix the radishes and half of the salt. Put the mixture in your Mortier Pilon fermentation jar and cover with the leaves and remaining salt. Let the mixture rest in the refrigerator for at least 3 days.

After the mixture has rested, place the garlic and ginger on a piece of cheesecloth. Tie the corners of the cheesecloth together to make a little bundle to be placed on the leaves.

Using a fork, make small holes in the hot peppers and add them to the jar along with the pears, scallions and onion. Cover with water and mix gently. Make sure to leave ¾ of an inch (2 centimeters) of headspace between the mixture and the rim of the jar.

Let the mixture ferment at room temperature, covered, for 3 days, at which time bubbles will have appeared on the surface. Serve or refrigerate.

To serve, place a generous serving of noodles in a bowl. Slice the fermented radishes into tiles and arrange them over the noodles, along with the other fermented ingredients (except for the bundle of garlic and ginger).

BIBIMBAP

(MIXED RICE)

This traditional Korean dish, whose name means mixed rice, is made with warm white rice, sautéed vegetables and gojuchang. Meat, mushrooms or a fried egg may also be added depending on who's preparing it. Served with kimchi on the side, this version is our tribute to tradition.

ACTIVE TIME

TOTAL TIME

INGREDIENTS

2 CLOVES **GARLIC**, CHOPPED

2 TBS (30 ML) **SUGAR**

4 TBS (60 ML) **SOY SAUCE**

2 TBS (30 ML) **RICE VINEGAR**

4 TBS (60 ML) **SESAME OIL**

12 OZ (350 G) **SIRLOIN STEAK**, CUT INTO THIN SLICES

3.5 OZ (100 G) **SHIITAKE MUSHROOMS**, SLICED

3 **CARROTS**, JULIENNED

6 BULBS **BOK CHOY**, ROUGHLY CHOPPED

2 TBS (30 ML) **GOCHUJANG**

4 **EGGS**

SALT AND **PEPPER**, TO TASTE

2 CUPS (500 ML) COOKED **JASMINE RICE**

SESAME SEEDS, FOR SERVING

CHOPPED **SCALLIONS**, FOR SERVING

KIMCHI BAECHU, FOR SERVING

KIMCHI KKAKDUGI, FOR SERVING

DIRECTIONS

In a large bowl, whisk together the garlic, sugar, soy sauce, rice vinegar and 1 tbs (15 ml) of sesame oil, until the sugar dissolves. Marinate the steak slices in the mixture for 20 minutes.

Meanwhile, sauté the mushrooms over medium-high heat in 1 tbs (15 ml) of sesame oil for 3 minutes. Transfer to a plate. Repeat this step with the carrots and transfer them to the same plate, making sure not to mix them with the mushrooms. Sauté the bok choy in 1 tbs (15 ml) of sesame oil for 3 minutes and transfer to the same plate.

Sauté the marinated meat, still over medium-high heat, in the remaining sesame oil for 3 to 5 minutes. Meanwhile, pan-fry the eggs.

To serve, divide the rice among 4 bowls and add the mushrooms, carrots, bok choy and meat. Top each bowl with a fried egg, sesame seeds and scallions. Serve with the kimchis.

SAU E K
R AU T™

Sauerkraut is to European cuisine—and, to a lesser extent, to North American cuisine—what kimchi is to Korea's culinary tradition: a delicious fermented food which bears both history and nutrients in large amounts. As early as 160 BC, Cato the Elder mentioned it in his De Agri Cultura, the oldest known work on agriculture.

However, it seems that the practice disappeared for a while after the fall of the Roman Empire. In fact, it took until the 13th century for it to be reintroduced in Europe, by way, the story goes, of Mongolian Emperor Genghis Khan's army, the campaigns of which not only took kimchi all over Eurasia, but more broadly, brought about a renewed interest in fermentation as a way to preserve food.

Sauerkraut's growing popularity quickly spread, causing new traditions to arise in each new country to which it traveled. Today, it is an integral part of the culinary heritage of Germany and France, as well as the Netherlands, and as far as Pennsylvania, where German immigrants popularized it practically from the day of their arrival in the 17th century.

TRADITIONAL SAUERKRAUT RECIPES

Sauerkraut enjoys a prominent place in European and American culinary repertoires. To truly learn about these cuisines, a good sauerkraut recipe, tasty and easy to prepare, is key.

TRADITIONAL EUROPEAN RECIPES

In Belorussian, Russian and Ukrainian cuisines, the cabbage is usually fermented with grated carrots; apples and cranberries may also be added. From Polish pierogi to Russian shchi and choucroute garnie, the following recipes include absolute musts of European cuisine—and they all feature sauerkraut!

TRADITIONAL AMERICAN RECIPES

Some recipes take inspiration from American cuisine to spotlight sauerkraut. The result is comforting, flavorful dishes that will make you want to sit down with your family and enjoy.

SAUER —

KRAUT

SIMPLE SAUERKRAUT

This is your basic sauerkraut, easy to prepare, customize and use as a base for many a meal inspired by European cuisine.

ACTIVE TIME   **TOTAL TIME**   **CROCK**   **FERMENTATION**

INGREDIENTS

4 KILOS **GREEN CABBAGE**, SHREDDED (ABOUT 4 HEADS)

6 TBS (90 ML) **COARSE SALT**

DIRECTIONS

Place the cabbage in your Mortier Pilon fermentation jar and press.

Cover with salt. Make sure to leave ¾ of an inch (2 centimeters) of headspace between the cabbage and the rim of the jar.

Let the mixture ferment at room temperature, covered, for at least 1 week. If, after 24 hours, the liquid that has appeared does not cover all of the cabbage, add some water and a pinch of salt.

Once the desired level of fermentation has been reached, refrigerate or serve.

BAVARIAN SAUERKRAUT

5 MIN	5 MIN	2L	1 WEEK
ACTIVE TIME	**TOTAL TIME**	**CROCK**	**FERMENTATION**

This sauerkraut is a popular, bulked-up alternative to traditional kraut. Contrary to what their name suggests, the Juniper berries which give it its distinct character are more a spice than an actual fruit. In season, you can find them fresh; during the rest of the year, you can buy them dried at your favorite specialty grocery store or health food store.

INGREDIENTS

4.5 LB (2 KILOS) **GREEN CABBAGE**, SHREDDED (ABOUT 2 HEADS)

2 **APPLES**, PEELED AND SLICED, OR ½ CUP (125 ML) APPLE JUICE

2 TBS (30 ML) WHOLE **CLOVES**

10 **JUNIPER BERRIES**

6 TBS (90 ML) **COARSE SALT**

DIRECTIONS

In a bowl, combine the cabbage, apples, cloves and juniper berries. Place the mixture in your Mortier Pilon fermentation jar and press.

Cover with salt. Make sure to leave ¾ of an inch (2 centimeters) of headspace between the cabbage mixture and the rim of the jar.

Let the mixture ferment at room temperature, covered, for at least 1 week. If, after 24 hours, the liquid that has appeared does not cover all of the cabbage, add some water and a pinch of salt.

Once the desired level of fermentation has been reached, refrigerate or serve.

SOUR SHCHI

30 MIN
ACTIVE TIME

1H45
TOTAL TIME

Both nutritious and bursting with flavor, shchi is the quintessential Russian soup. This affordable, easy to make dish will no doubt become a staple of your winter repertoire. The traditional first course of Russian meals for over a thousand years, its main ingredient is cabbage, often in sauerkraut form, in which case the dish is called sour shchi.

INGREDIENTS

1 CUP (250 ML) DRIED **PORCINI MUSHROOMS**

2 SMALL **POTATOES**, CUBED

3 CUPS (750 ML) **SIMPLE SAUERKRAUT**

4 TBS (60 ML) **VEGETABLE OIL**

¼ CUP (65 ML) **WATER**

2 **CARROTS**, CUT INTO ROUNDS

2 FRESH **TOMATOES**, SEEDED AND CHOPPED

1 LARGE **ONION**, CHOPPED

½ CUP (125 ML) FRESH **PARSLEY LEAVES**

1 STALK **CELERY**, SLICED

1 TSP (5 ML) **SALT**

½ TSP (2.5 ML) **SUGAR**

FRESH **PARSLEY**, **DILL** AND **SOUR CREAM** FOR SERVING (OPTIONAL)

DIRECTIONS

Rehydrate the mushrooms by soaking them in a bowl filled with water for at least 1 hour.

While the mushrooms are soaking, boil the potatoes. Wring out the sauerkraut by hand and pulse it for several seconds in a food processor until finely chopped. Heat in a pan until tender. Add 2 tbs (30 ml) of oil and the water and stir together. Cover the pan and set aside.

Drain the rehydrated mushrooms and reserve the soaking water. Cut the mushrooms into thin strips. Heat the rest of the oil in a large saucepan. Sauté the mushrooms for 5 minutes. Gradually blend in the sauerkraut, soaking water, potatoes, carrots, tomatoes, onion, parsley, celery, salt and sugar.

Let the soup simmer for 30 minutes. Add some water if it seems too thick. Serve with fresh herbs and sour cream.

POLISH PIEROGI

Considered by many as Poland's national dish, pierogi exist in many varieties, each suited to a particular taste or occasion; salty as an appetizer or as part of an entrée, and sweet for dessert. Our version is stuffed with onions, sour cream and kraut, and is inspired by the pierogi served as part of the traditional Christmas meal.

ACTIVE TIME 45 MIN

TOTAL TIME 1H00

INGREDIENTS

2 ½ CUPS (625 ML) **SIMPLE SAUERKRAUT**

1 ½ CUPS (375 ML) CHOPPED **ONIONS**

3 TBS (45 ML) **LARD**

¼ CUP (65 ML) **SOUR CREAM**

½ TSP (2.5 ML) **SALT**

½ TSP (2.5 ML) **PEPPER**

3 CUPS (750 ML) ALL-PURPOSE **FLOUR**

1 TBS (15 ML) **SALT**

1 COLD LARGE **EGG**

3 TBS (45 ML) **VEGETABLE OIL**

1 CUP (250 ML) WARM **WATER**

SOUR CREAM, **BACON** AND **CHIVES**, FOR SERVING

DIRECTIONS

Wring out the sauerkraut by hand and pulse it for several seconds in a food processor until finely chopped. Set aside.

In a saucepan, sauté the onions in the lard for 3 minutes. Add the sauerkraut, sour cream, pepper and ½ tsp (2.5 ml) salt. Stir. Bring to a boil, then let simmer for 10 minutes, or until the mixture becomes thick and sticky. Remove from heat and let cool.

Meanwhile, in a bowl combine the flour and 1 tsp (5 ml) salt. Add the egg, oil and water. Mix until a dough forms.

Flour a clean and clear work surface. Lay down the dough onto the prepared surface. Knead the dough until it is no longer sticky. (Make sure not to over-knead the dough, as this will toughen it.) Using your hands, roll the kneaded dough into a ball and place it in a bowl. Cover and let rest at room temperature for 15 minutes.

After the dough has rested, turn it back out onto the floured surface. Using a rolling pin, roll out the dough into a ¼-inch (5-millimeter) thick disk. Using a circular pastry cutter or water glass, cut the dough into circles.

Place 2 tbs (30 ml) of stuffing in the center of each circle. Moisten the edge with a little water and fold each circle in half to make a half-moon shape. Set the pierogi aside on a floured surface. Cover with a clean, damp kitchen towel to prevent them from drying out. Lightly oil a baking sheet or dish.

Bring a large pot of salted water to a boil. Place several pierogi in the water. Cook for 5 or 10 minutes, or until the pierogi are plump and rise to the surface. Cooking time may vary depending on the size of the pierogi. Once the pierogi have cooked, gently remove them from the boiling water (preferably using a slotted spoon) and place them on the oiled tray. Cover with a cloth or a sheet of aluminum foil. Repeat until all the pierogi are cooked.

If possible, keep the pierogi hot until serving time. You may also reheat the pierogi over low heat in a pan with butter or oil, or steam them in a steamer basket. Serve with sour cream, bacon and chives.

CHOUCROUTE GARNIE

(DRESSED SAUERKRAUT)

ACTIVE TIME 1H15

TOTAL TIME 1H30

Choucroute garnie became a French favorite shortly after Alsace-Lorraine was annexed to France in the 17th century. The sauerkraut cooks slowly alongside sausages and cured meats and is served with potatoes. Though traditional, this remains a versatile dish, so feel free to add fresh herbs, onions or apple slices if you'd like.

INGREDIENTS

4 SMALL **HAM HOCKS**

4 **BRATWURST-STYLE SAUSAGES**, COOKED

12 THICK SLICES **BACON**, DICED

2 CUPS (500 ML) **ONION**, CHOPPED

10 JUNIPER BERRIES

10 WHOLE **CLOVES**

2 WHOLE **BAY LEAVES**

2 **APPLES**, PEELED AND DICED

4 CUPS (1L) **SIMPLE SAUERKRAUT**, WRUNG OUT

2 **KIELBASA-STYLE SAUSAGES**, DICED

6 **KNACKWURST SAUSAGES**, DICED

1½ CUPS (375 ML) DRY **WHITE WINE**

8 NEW **POTATOES**

½ CUP (125 ML) FRESH **PARSLEY**, ROUGHLY CHOPPED

DIJON MUSTARD OR **HORSERADISH**, FOR SERVING

DIRECTIONS

Place the ham hocks in a large pan and cover with water. Bring to a boil and let simmer for 2 hours, or until the meat is very tender. Remove the ham hocks from the pan and let cool. Reserve the stock. When the ham hocks have cooled, remove the meat from the bone and set aside. (At this step, you can throw away the bones.)

In the same pan, boil the stock until it is reduced by half or until about 2 cups (500 ml) of liquid remain. Reserve.

Preheat the oven to 350°F (175°C). In a large pan, cook the sausages and bacon over medium-high heat for about 10 minutes. Set aside the cooked sausages. In the same pan, sauté the onions, juniper berries and bay leaves until the onions are translucent. Add the apples and continue cooking until they are tender. Add the sauerkraut, all the meat, the wine and the reduced stock. Bring to a boil, then let simmer for 10 minutes.

After 10 minutes, transfer to a baking dish and for about 90 minutes. Meanwhile, boil the potatoes in salted water until they are tender. Drain the potatoes and transfer to a serving dish. Garnish with parsley.

Arrange the meat and sauerkraut on a serving platter. Serve with the potatoes and Dijon mustard or horseradish.

VEPŘO-KNEDLO-ZELO

(ROAST PORK WITH DUMPLINGS AND SAUERKRAUT)

Even though this dish is also eaten in Austria and Bavaria, only the Czech gave it a name of its own. As the name, which literally means pork-dumplings-cabbage, indicates, the dish combines bread dumplings, cooked sauerkraut and pork roast—all three of them staples of Czech cuisine.

ACTIVE TIME

TOTAL TIME

INGREDIENTS

FOR THE PORK ROAST:

2 TBS (30 ML) OLIVE OIL

1 TSP (5 ML) DIJON MUSTARD

2 TSP (10 ML) WHOLE CARAWAY SEEDS

2 CLOVES GARLIC, CHOPPED

1 TSP (5 ML) SALT

1½ TSP (7.5 ML) GROUND BLACK PEPPER

2 LB (1 KILO) PORK LOIN

2 SMALL ONIONS, CHOPPED

⅔ CUP (170 ML) CHICKEN STOCK

1 TSP (5 ML) CORNSTARCH
DILUTED IN 2 TSP (10 ML) COLD WATER

2 TSP (10 ML) SALTED BUTTER

FOR THE DUMPLINGS:

2 TSP (10 ML) BAKER'S YEAST

1 TBS (15 ML) CANE SUGAR

1 CUP (250 ML) MILK

1 EGG

A PINCH SALT

2 CUPS (500 ML) ALL-PURPOSE FLOUR

1½ CUPS (375 ML) WHITE BREAD,
CRUSTS REMOVED AND CUT INTO CUBES

FOR THE CABBAGE:

3 CUPS (750 ML) SIMPLE SAUERKRAUT

2 TSP (10 ML) BUTTER

100 GRAMS SALTED LARD, CUT INTO SMALL CUBES

1 SMALL ONION, CHOPPED

½ TSP (2.5 ML) GROUND CUMIN SEEDS

4 TSP (20 ML) CANE SUGAR

½ TSP (2.5 ML) SALT

½ TSP (2.5 ML) PEPPER

1 TSP (5 ML) CORNSTARCH
DILUTED IN 2 TSP (10 ML) COLD WATER

DIRECTIVES

For the pork roast:

In a small bowl, combine the oil, Dijon mustard, caraway seeds, garlic, salt and pepper. Rub the pork loin with the spice mixture. Let marinate for 1 hour in the refrigerator.

Preheat the oven to 350°F (175°C). Place the onions in a large roasting pan and cover with the chicken stock. After the pork loin has rested, place it in the roasting pan, on top of the onions. Cover with a sheet of aluminum foil. Roast in the oven for 3 hours. After one hour, turn the pork loin and continue roasting, uncovered. Baste frequently throughout the cooking time.

Once the pork has cooked, remove it from the roasting pan (reserve the liquid) and let rest for 10 minutes before slicing. Transfer the cooking juices to a small saucepan and bring to a boil. Whisk in the butter and diluted cornstarch and let simmer until the mixture thickens. Lower the heat and keep the sauce hot until serving time.

For the dumplings:

In a large bowl, mix together the yeast and sugar with ½ a cup (125 ml) milk. Let rest for 10 minutes. Add the remaining milk along with the egg, salt and flour. Knead for about 10 minutes, until the mixture achieves an elastic texture. Incorporate the bread cubes and knead. Cover the dough with a clean cloth and let it rest for 2 hours in a warm place (for example, in the oven, turned off but with the light on). The dough should double in volume.

Knead the dough once again and divide into 2 pieces. Using a rolling pin, roll out each piece of dough into a cylinder measuring 1.5 inches (4 centimeters) in diameter. Let the 2 cylinders of dough rise for 30 minutes.

Fill a large pot with water and add salt. Place the first cylinder in the pot. Cover and let boil for 10 minutes without lifting the lid. Carefully remove the cylinder from the boiling water and place it on a cutting board. Pierce the cylinder with a knife or fork to make small holes that will let steam escape. Wrap the dough in a damp cloth. Repeat with the other dough cylinder. Just before serving, slice each cylinder to make ¾-inch (2-centimeter) thick disks.

For the sauerkraut:

Wring out the sauerkraut and reserve the juice. Chop the sauerkraut into strips approximately 4 centimeters long. Set aside.

In a pan, melt the butter and brown the lard and onion. Add the cumin and sauerkraut and cook for 2 minutes. Add the sauerkraut, sugar, salt and pepper. Mix. Bring to a boil, then let simmer, covered, for 10 minutes.

If, after 10 minutes, the mixture is too watery, thicken by adding the diluted cornstarch. Serve immediately with the roast pork and dumplings.

PENNSYLVANIA-STYLE PORK ROAST

ACTIVE TIME 15 MIN

TOTAL TIME 3H00

We owe the Pennsylvania Dutch not only the American popularity of pretzels, but also this dish made of pork and sauerkraut, which is traditionally served steaming hot on a large plate at the center of the table.

INGREDIENTS

1 TSP (5 ML) DEHYDRATED **ONION**

2 TSP (10 ML) **GARLIC SALT**

1 TSP (5 ML) **MUSTARD SEEDS**, GROUND

2 TSP (10 ML) **WORCESTERSHIRE SAUCE**
OR **RED WINE VINEGAR**

A PINCH GROUND **BLACK PEPPER**

2 KILOS **PORK LOIN**

3 CUPS (750 ML) **SIMPLE SAUERKRAUT**,
WRUNG OUT

A PINCH **SUGAR**

1 **SMOKED SAUSAGE**, CUT INTO ROUNDS

DIJON MUSTARD OR **HORSERADISH**, FOR SERVING

DIRECTIONS

Preheat the oven to 350°F (175°C).

In a small bowl, mix together the dehydrated onion, garlic salt, mustard seeds, Worcestershire sauce and pepper.

Place the pork loin in a dutch oven and rub it with the spice mixture. Cover with the sauerkraut and sugar.

Roast the pork in the oven, covered, for about 2 and a half hours, or until a meat thermometer registers an internal temperature of 160°F (71°C). While you wait, heat the sauerkraut on low heat in a pot.

Remove the roast from the oven. Cover with aluminum foil and let stand 15 minutes before serving. Serve with sauerkraut, smoked sausage and garnish with dijon mustard or horseradish.

COUNTRY-STYLE KRAUT & RIBS

ACTIVE TIME

TOTAL TIME

The key to making this no-fuss but flavorful dish a success is patience, especially as the meat cooks slowly in the oven among humble but hand-picked ingredients, as quality and simplicity are the distinctive features of this recipe.

INGREDIENTS

1 KILO **PORK SPARE RIBS**, BONE-IN

1 SMALL **YELLOW ONION**, CHOPPED

1 TSP (5 ML) **VEGETABLE OIL**

2 CUPS (500 ML) **SIMPLE SAUERKRAUT**, WRUNG OUT

2 **APPLES,** PEELED AND DICED

4 TSP (20 ML) **CANE SUGAR**

1 TBS (15 ML) GROUND **CORIANDER SEEDS**

1 SMALL CLOVE **GARLIC**, CHOPPED

A PINCH GROUND **BLACK PEPPER**

DIRECTIONS

Preheat the oven to 350°F (175°C).

In a cast iron dutch oven, cook the pork ribs and the onion in the oil until golden brown. Remove from heat and set aside.

In a bowl, mix together the sauerkraut, apples, sugar, coriander seeds, garlic and pepper. Cover the pork ribs with the sauerkraut mixture. Cook in the oven, covered, for 90 minutes.

CLASSIC REUBEN SANDWICH

A true classic in American delis, traditionally made with slices of roast beef, Swiss cheese and sauerkraut, this sandwich is truly bursting with flavor. Served on rye with a homemade Russian dressing, our version aims to be a tribute to tradition.

ACTIVE TIME   **TOTAL TIME**

INGREDIENTS

¼ CUP (65 ML) **MAYONNAISE**

3 TSP (15 ML) **CHILI SAUCE**

1 SMALL **PICKLE**, FINELY CHOPPED

A PINCH **SALT**

A PINCH **PEPPER**

8 SLICES WHOLE GRAIN **RYE BREAD**

4 SLICES **EMMENTAL CHEESE**

4 SLICES **HAVARTI CHEESE**

24 THIN SLICES **ROAST BEEF**

24 THIN SLICES OF YOUR FAVORITE **SMOKED MEAT**

2 CUPS (500 ML) **SIMPLE SAUERKRAUT**, WRUNG OUT

4 TSP (20 ML) **VEGETABLE OIL**

4 SLICED **PICKLES**, FOR SERVING

DIRECTIONS

In a small bowl, combine the mayonnaise, chili sauce, chopped pickle, salt and pepper.

Place 4 slices of bread on a baking sheet. Cover each slice with 1 tablespoon of the Russian sauce prepared in the previous step. Add to each slice of bread 1 slice Emmental, 1 slice Havarti, 6 slices roast beef and 6 slices smoked meat. Divide the remaining Russian sauce among the 4 sandwiches. Top each sandwich with a slice of bread.

Heat half of the oil over medium heat in a large nonstick pan. Toast 2 sandwiches in the pan at a time, for 3 minutes on each side. Repeat with the remaining oil and sandwiches. Serve with the sliced pickles.

MOLECULAR RECIPES

TIPS & TRICKS

R-EVOLUTION D.I.Y. KITS

REFILLS & ACCESSORIES

MOLECULE-R.COM

MORTIER PILON
PHOTOGRAPHY BY
SYLVIE RACICOT
CHEZVALOIS.COM